SONG OF THE SUN

*A Birthday Song
for William H. Hastings Jr.
June 15 - 1954 -*

E. E. -

SONG OF THE SUN

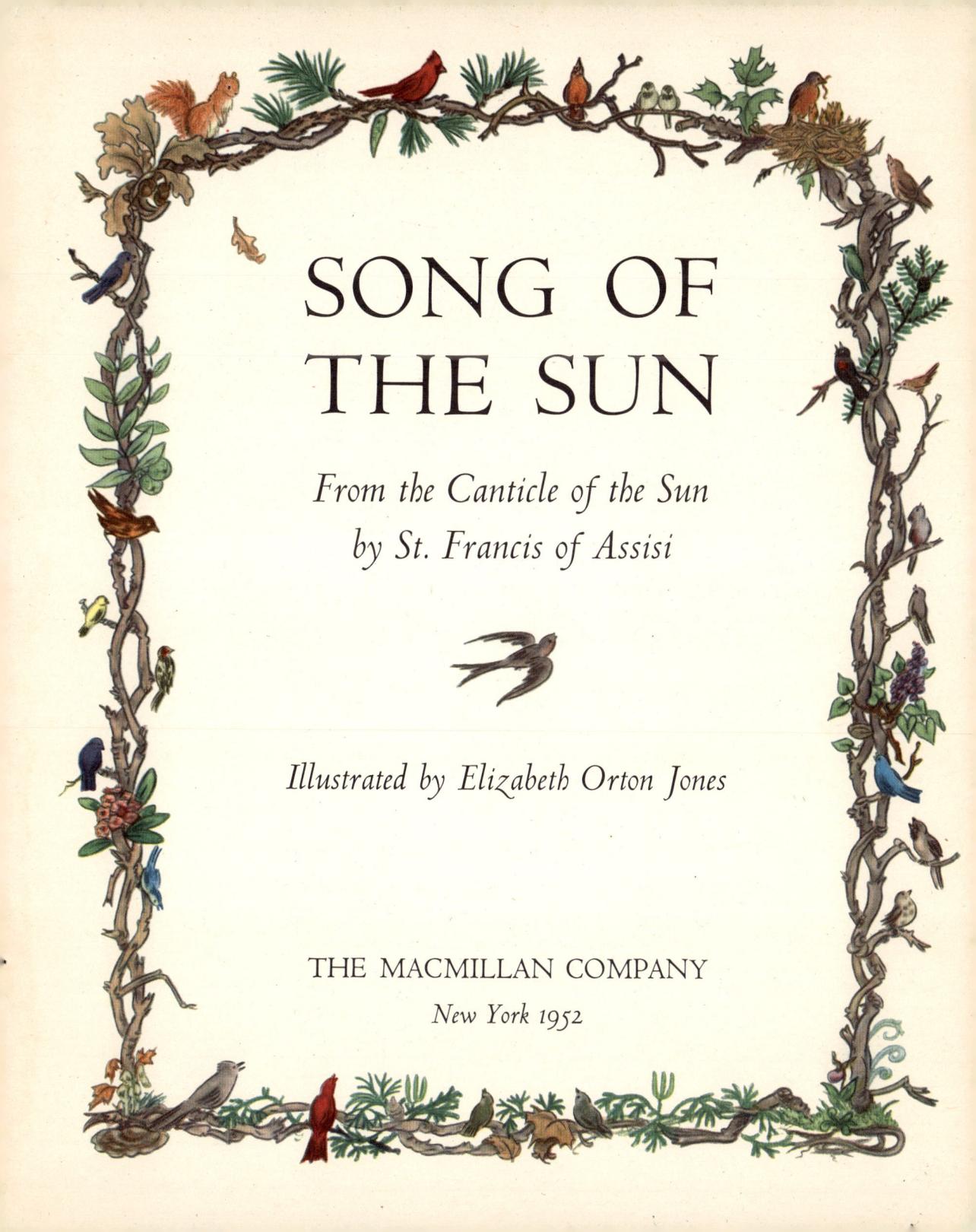

From the Canticle of the Sun
by St. Francis of Assisi

Illustrated by Elizabeth Orton Jones

THE MACMILLAN COMPANY
New York 1952

FOR HADLEY

COPYRIGHT, 1952, BY THE MACMILLAN COMPANY

All rights reserved—no part of this book may be reproduced in any form without permission in writing from the publisher, except by a reviewer who wishes to quote brief passages in connection with a review written for inclusion in magazine or newspaper.

First Printing

PRINTED IN THE UNITED STATES OF AMERICA

Long ago there lived a man who sang a song, not only with his voice but with his whole life, a man who called all things his brothers and sisters: the sun and the moon, water, fire and wind; a man whose heart was full of joy, full of love for all things, and full of praise to God who made all things. His name was Francis. Saint Francis, we call him today—Saint Francis of Assisi, because the town of Assisi, in Italy, is where he was born.

Many people have little statues of Saint Francis in their gardens, where birds come and flowers grow. I have one, too—in a little shelter which is nailed to a tree. The little shelter is brown, but the part behind Saint Francis is painted blue because, I think, the sky behind the town of Assisi, in Italy, is always very blue. On the floor of the little shelter, around Saint Francis' feet, I put seeds and crumbs and things birds like to eat, especially in winter. And birds come. Squirrels come, too. They seem to feel that they are welcome. They seem to know this little man, this great man, who talked to them and tamed them, and hoped that no one would catch them or kill them or do them any harm.

Indeed, he used to preach sermons to his little sisters, the birds. Once he went into a field and began to preach to a great many birds who were there on the ground. And those that were on the trees flew down to hear him, too. And they all stood still and listened, while he told them that they ought always and in every place, to praise God and be thankful to Him. While he was speaking the birds opened their beaks and stretched their necks and spread their wings and bowed their heads. And when his sermon was ended, they all flew up into the air singing.

Once a little captured rabbit was brought to him which was very wild and wanted to escape. But no sooner did the little rabbit see Saint Francis, than it jumped into his arms and nestled close against him. Saint Francis spoke to it gently, telling it to beware of being captured again; then he set it on the ground to let it go. But the little rabbit no longer wanted to escape. It jumped again into Saint Francis' arms, and he carried it around with him, and it became very tame.

And once a lamb was brought to him. He taught it to go to church, so that whenever it heard the bells ringing or the choir singing the lamb would enter the church by itself, and bend its knees and bow its head.

And once Saint Francis met a boy who had caught some wild turtle-doves and was taking them to market to sell. Saint Francis begged the boy to give the birds to him, and when he did Saint Francis took them home and tamed them and made nests for them all, and they stayed and laid eggs in the nests and were, to him, like chickens.

And once, near a certain city called Gubbio, there was a wolf so huge and terrible that people feared for their lives, and no man dared to go anywhere unless he was armed as if he were

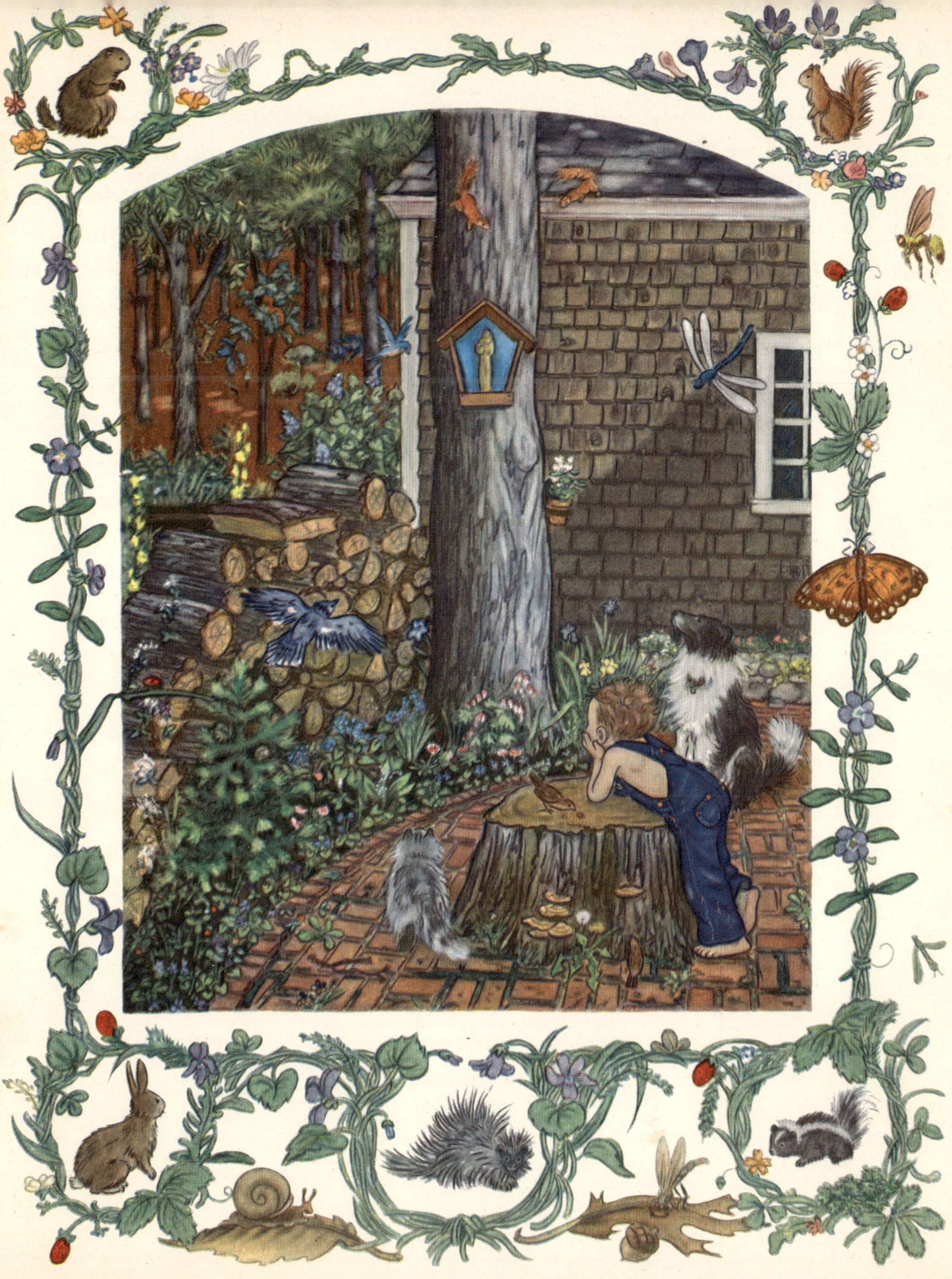

going to battle. But Saint Francis went, without any weapon, to where the wolf was; and when the wolf came to meet him he said, "Brother Wolf, I come to make peace with you. If you will promise me to hurt neither man nor beast, I will promise you that the people of this city will feed you, so that you will never go hungry. Do you promise?" The wolf lifted his right paw and gently laid it in Saint Francis' hand. Then, together they went back to the city. And from that day he was a tame wolf, going in and out of the houses, hurting no one, and no one hurt him. And he was kindly fed by all the people. And when Brother Wolf died, at a very old age, they were all very sad, for they had come to love him dearly.

There are many stories about Saint Francis. I hope you will read them all, some day. And there is a beautiful prayer of his which I hope you will know. But now—listen to the words of the song he sang and left here in the world for us to sing, too.

Song of the Sun we call it—or *The Song of Brother Sun*. Sometimes it is called *The Canticle of the Sun,* and sometimes *The Canticle of the Creatures.* Canticle means song; not just an ordinary song, but a song of praise. And that is just what his song is: praise to God for all things, by all creatures.

Listen—not only with your ears but with your whole self. Let the song become part of you. Let the love and the joy Saint Francis felt be your love and joy, too.

Mason, New Hampshire   E.O.J.

SONG OF THE SUN

O most high almighty, good Lord God, to Thee belong praise, glory, honour, and all blessing!

Praised be my Lord God with all His creatures; and specially our brother the sun, who brings us the day, and who brings us the light; fair is he, and shining with a very great splendour.

Praised be my Lord for our sister the moon, and for the stars the which He has set clear and lovely in heaven.

Praised be my Lord for our brother the wind, and for air and cloud, calms and all weather, by the which Thou upholdest in life all creatures.

Praised be my Lord for our sister water, who is very serviceable unto us, and humble, and precious, and clean.

Praised be my Lord for our brother fire, through whom Thou givest us light in the darkness; and he is bright and pleasant, and very mighty, and strong.

Praised be my Lord for our mother the earth, the which doth sustain us and keep us, and bringeth forth divers fruits, and flowers of many colours, and grass.

Praise ye, and bless ye the Lord, and give thanks unto Him and serve Him with great humility.

O MOST high, almighty, good Lord God, to Thee belong praise, glory, honour, and all blessing!

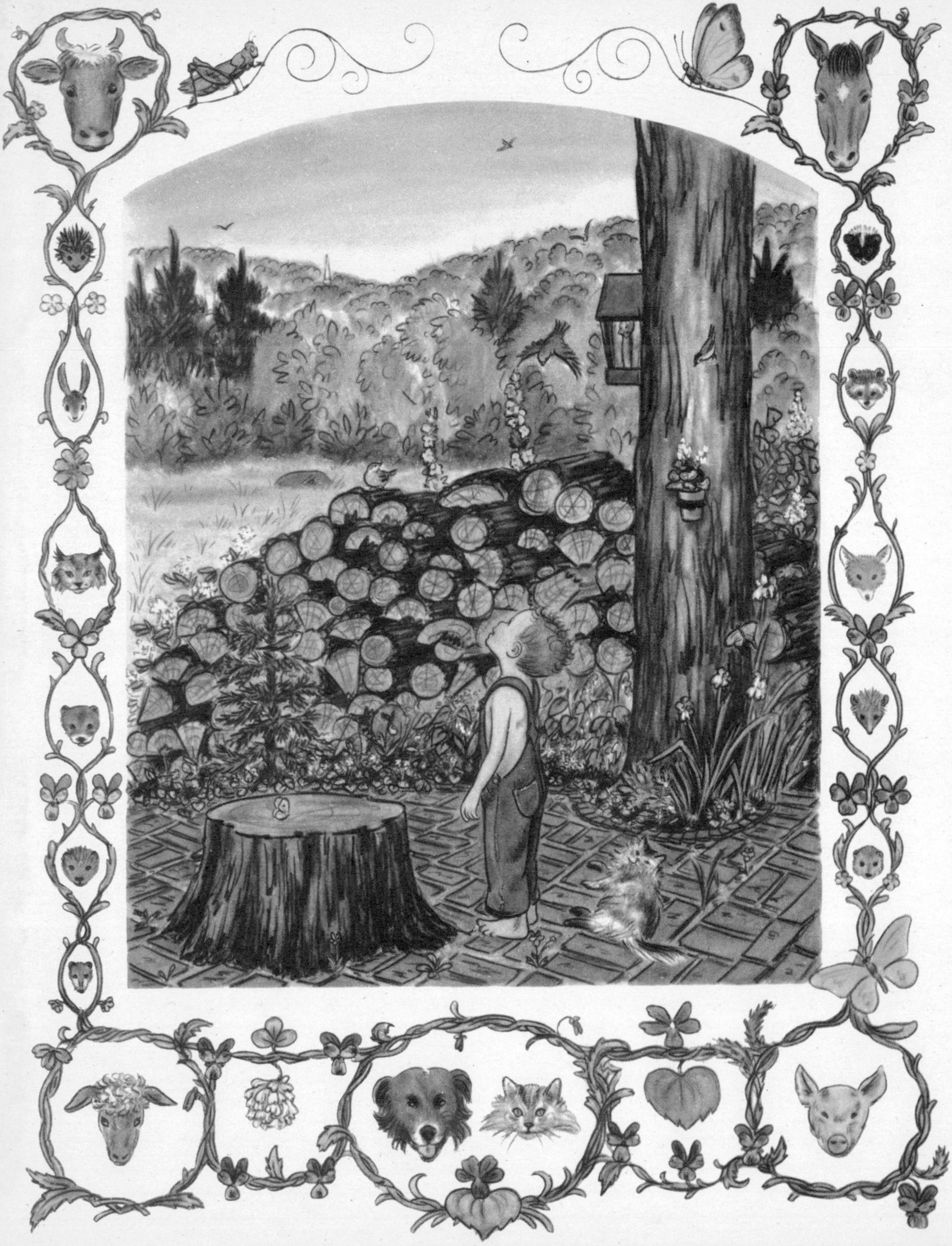

PRAISED be my Lord God with all His creatures; and specially our brother the sun, who brings us the day, and who brings us the light; fair is he, and shining with a very great splendour.

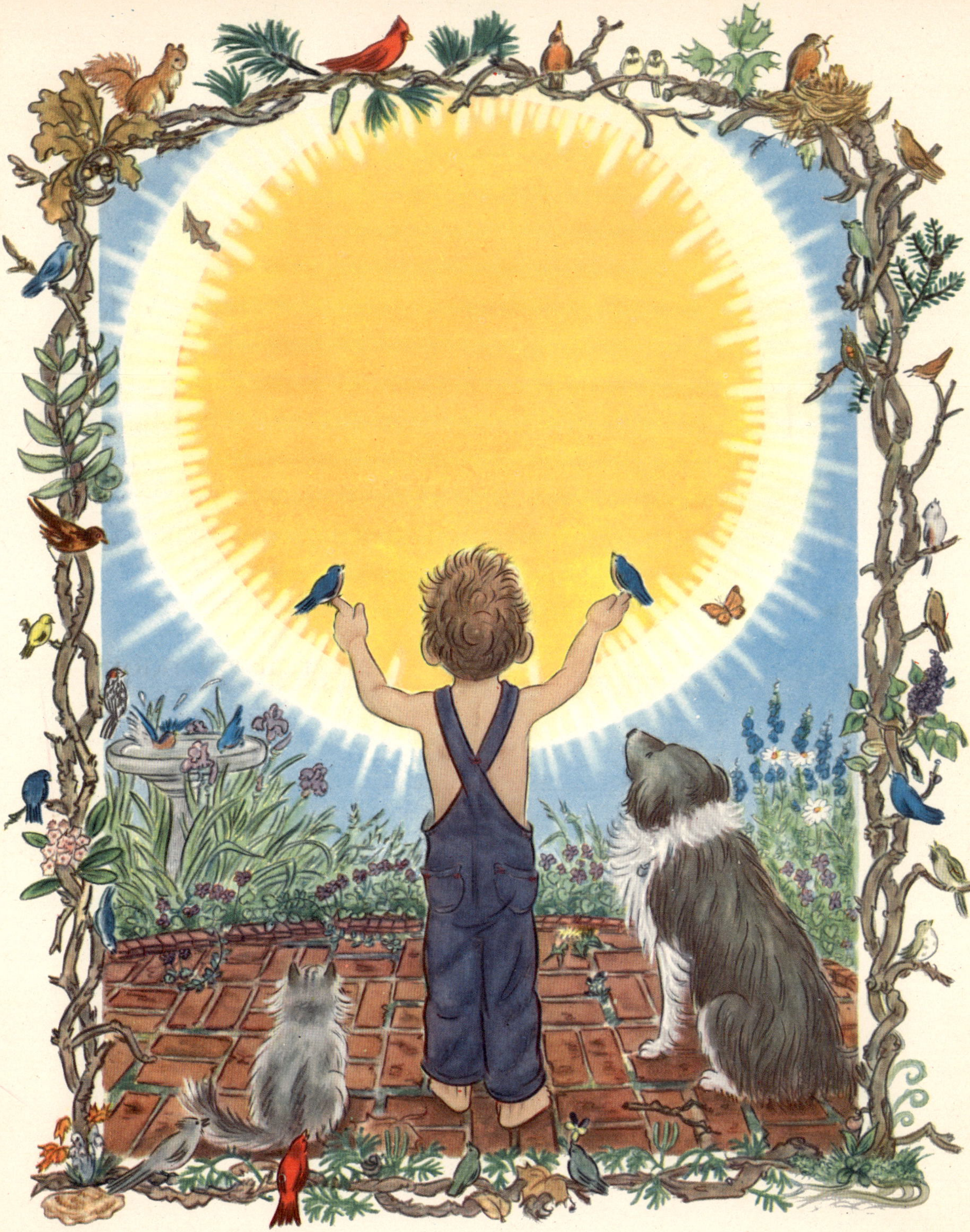

PRAISED be my Lord for our sister the moon, and for the stars the which He has set clear and lovely in heaven.

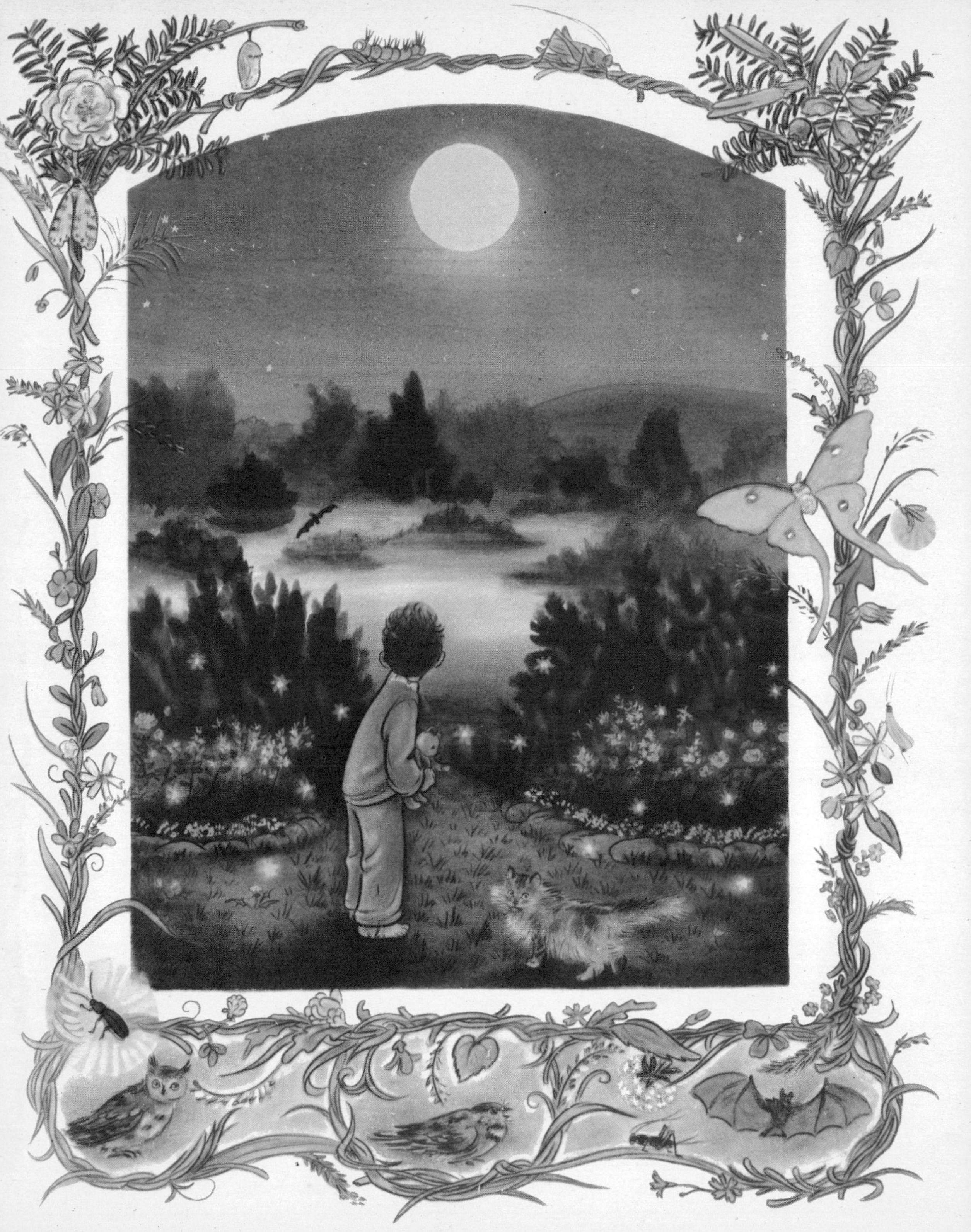

PRAISED be my Lord for our brother the wind, and for air and cloud, calms and all weather, by the which Thou upholdest in life all creatures.

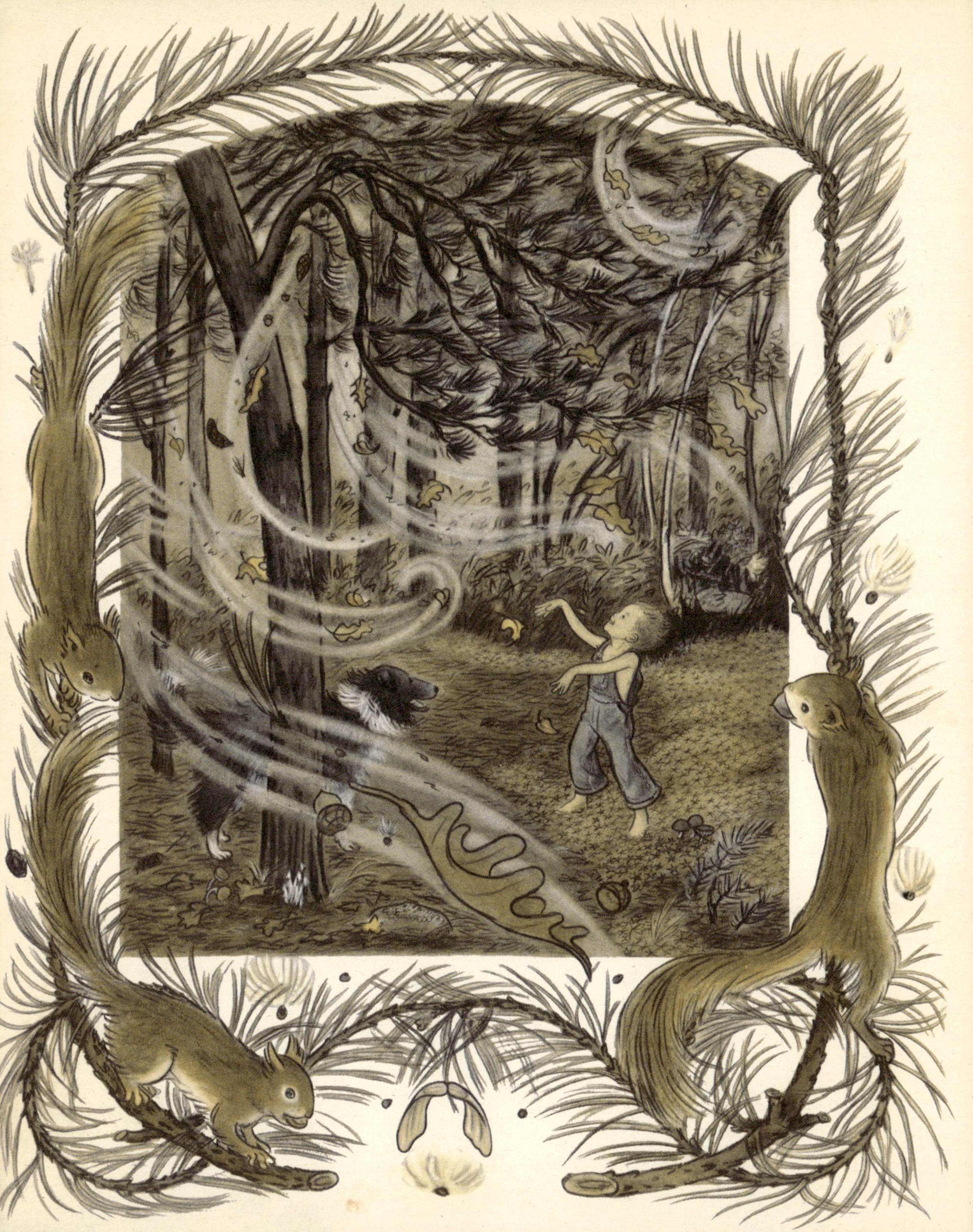

PRAISED be my Lord for our sister water, who is very serviceable unto us, and humble, and precious, and clean.

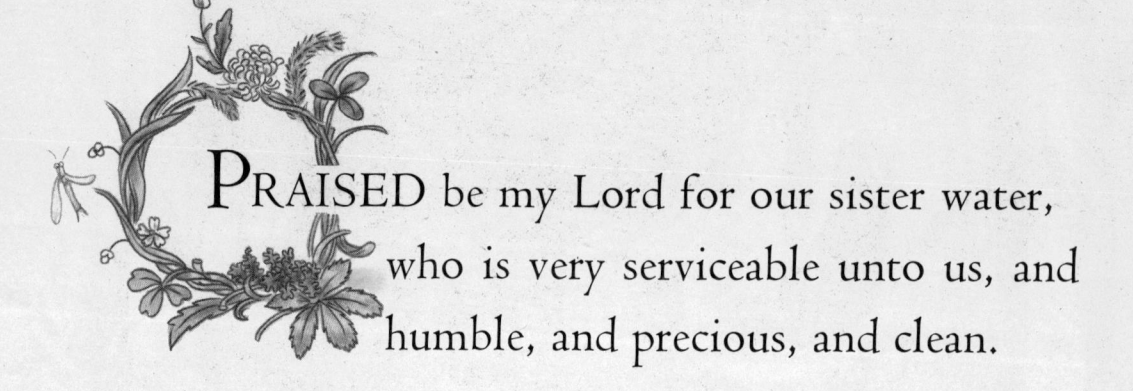

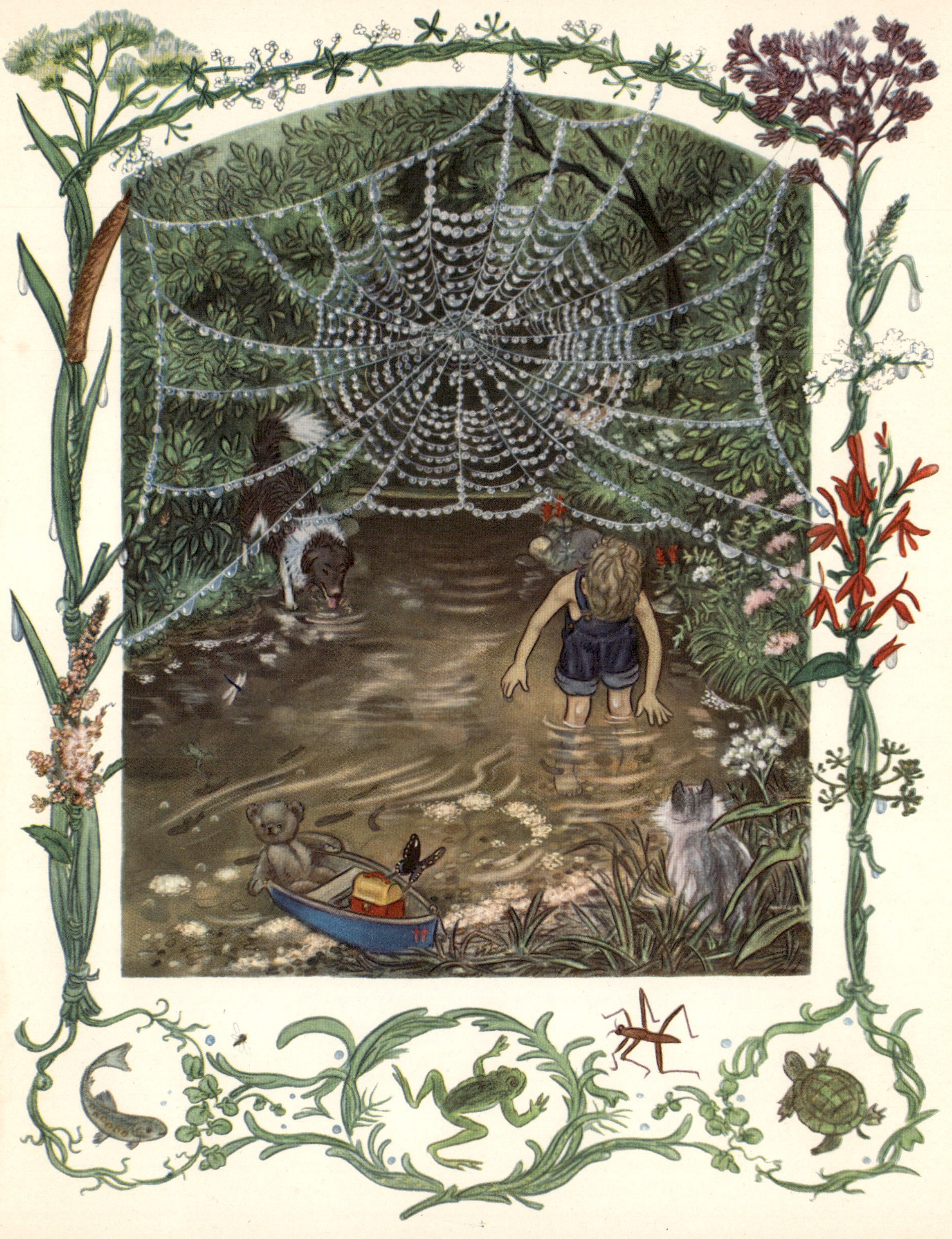

PRAISED be my Lord for our brother fire, through whom Thou givest us light in the darkness; and he is bright and pleasant, and very mighty, and strong.

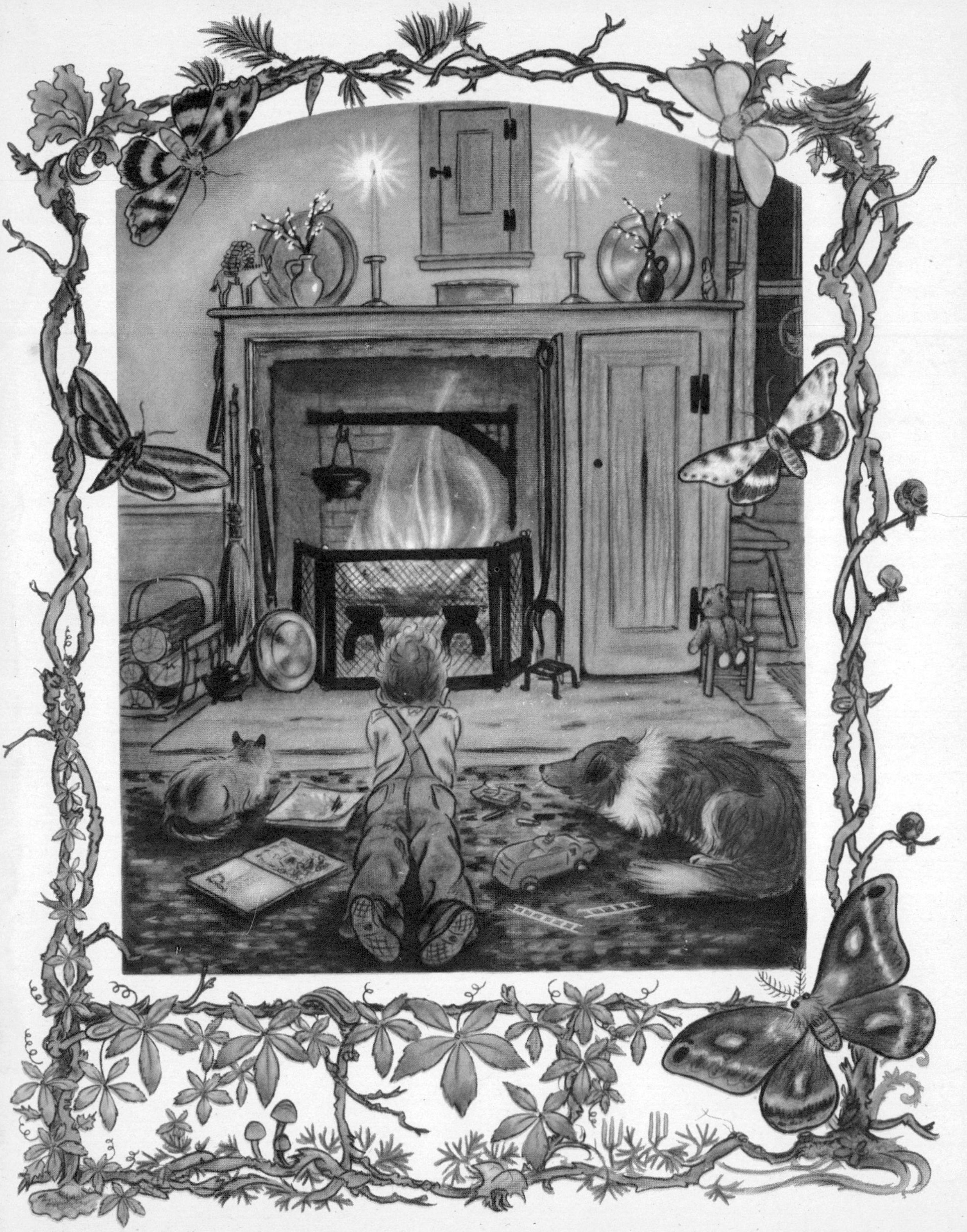

PRAISED be my Lord for our mother the earth, the which doth sustain us and keep us, and bringeth forth divers fruits, and flowers of many colours, and grass.

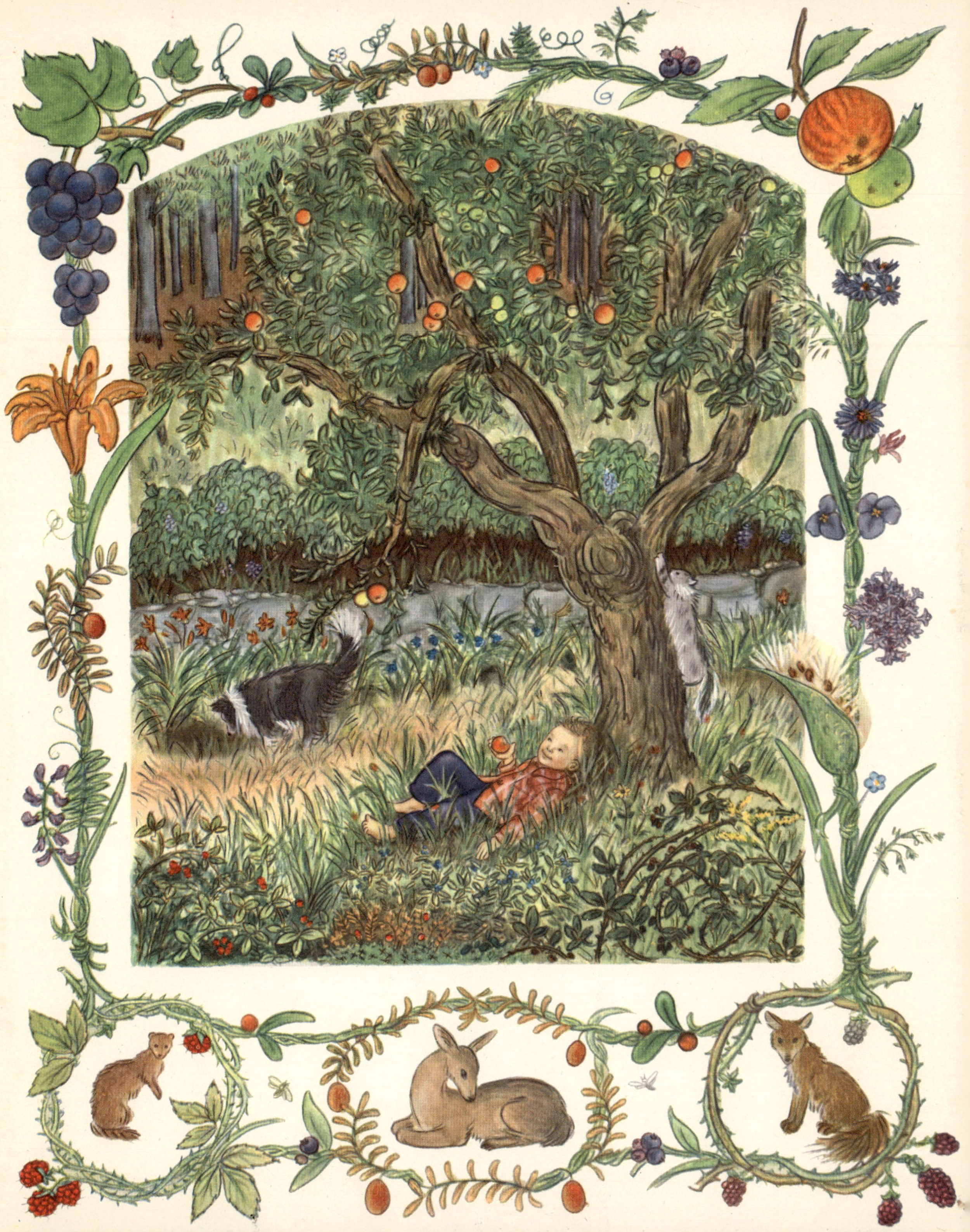

PRAISE ye, and bless ye the Lord,

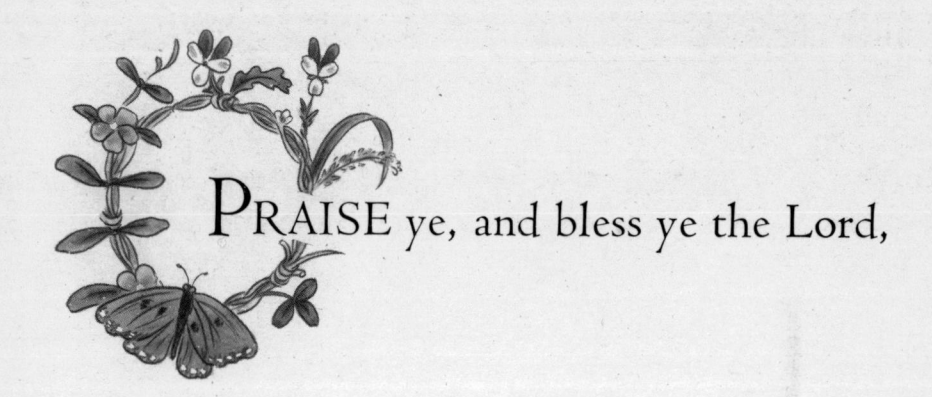

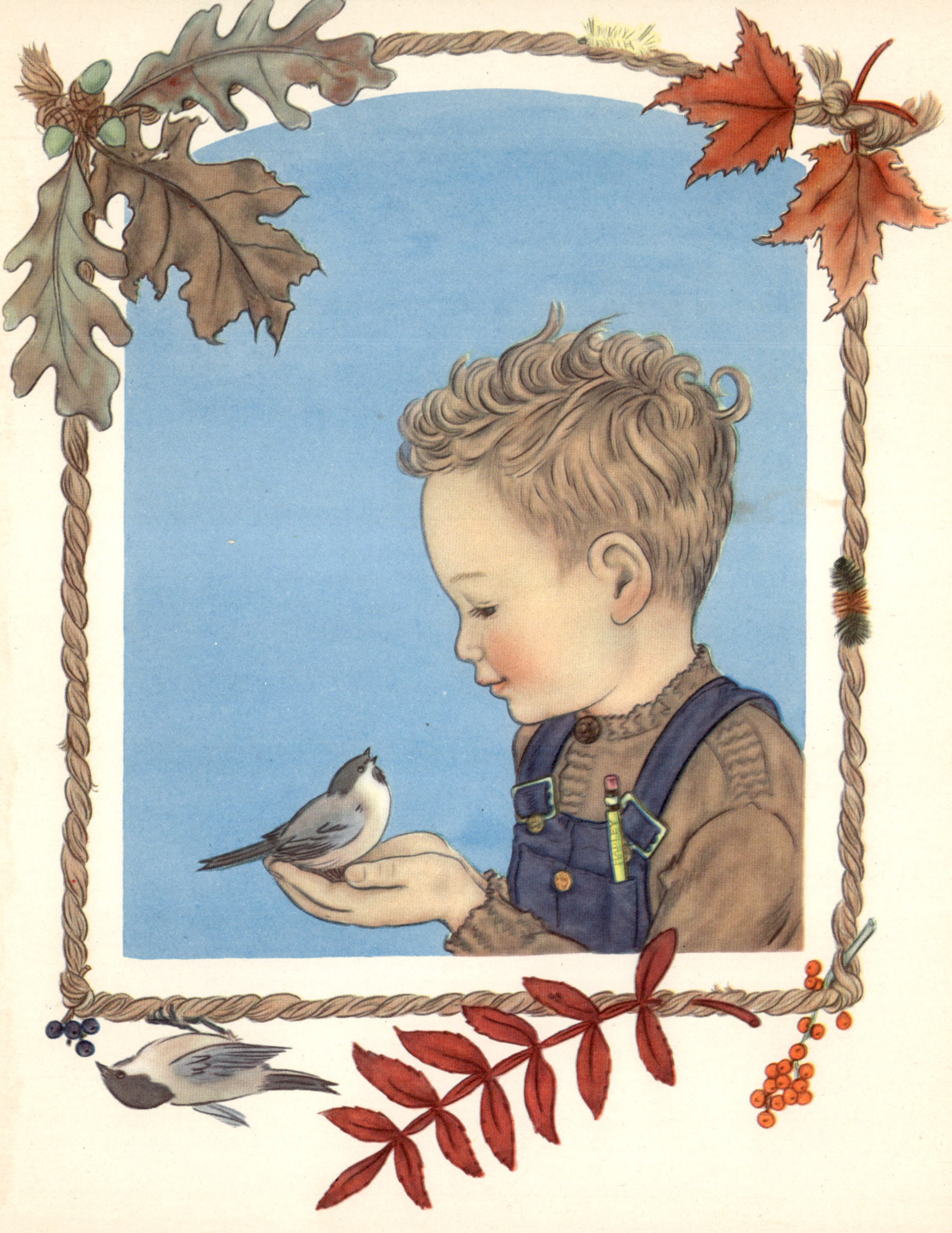

AND give thanks unto Him

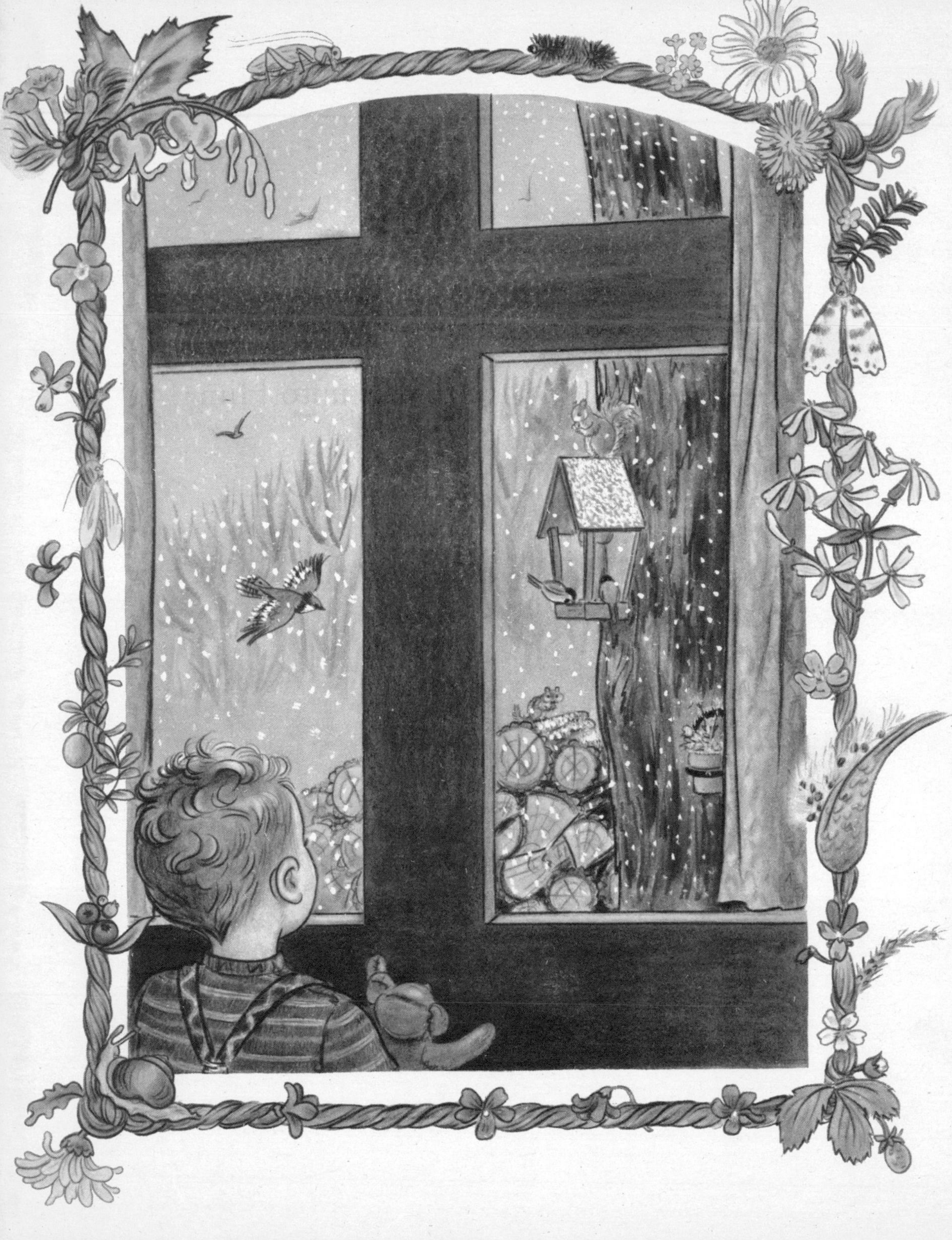

AND serve Him with great humility.

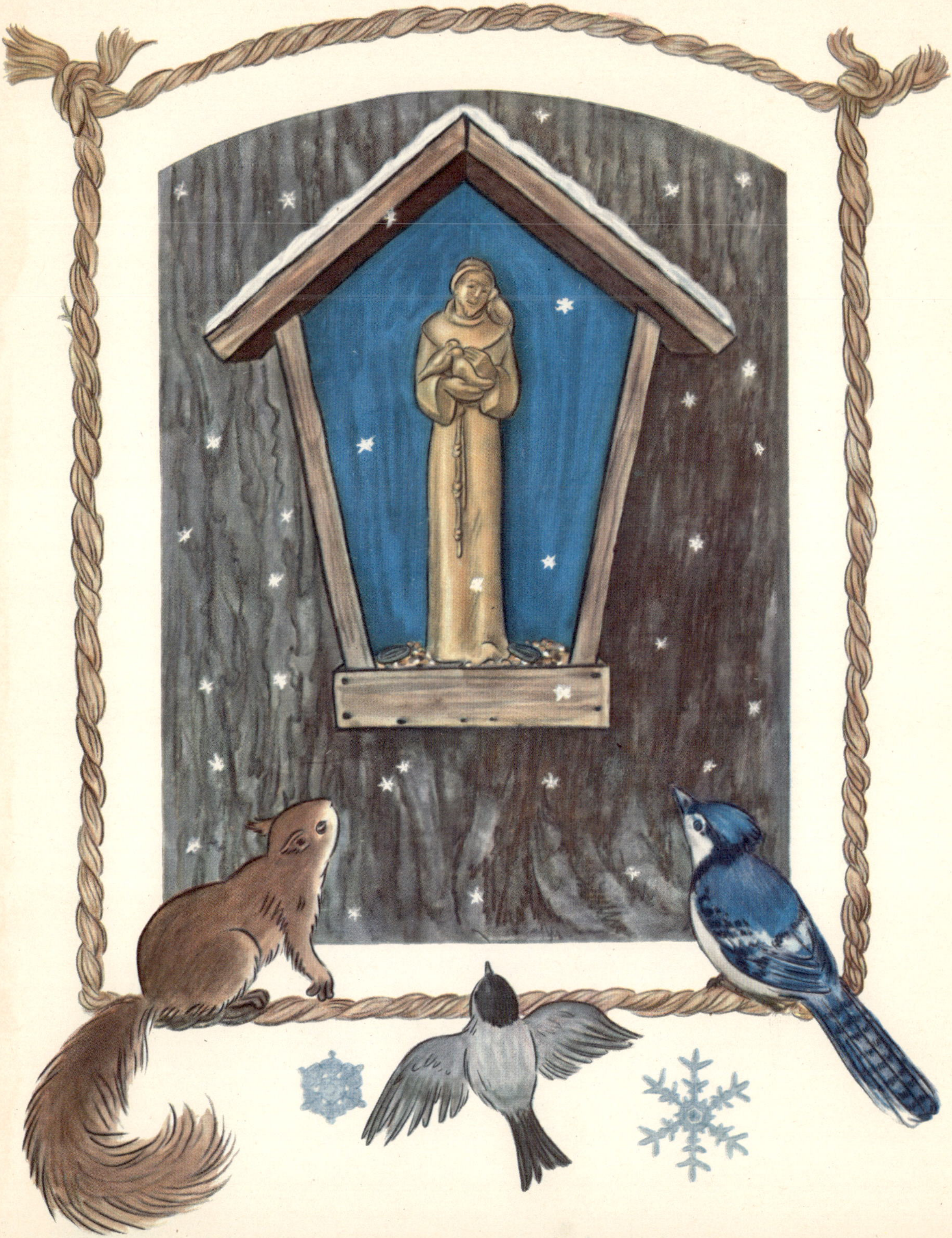

Some day, perhaps, you will visit the town of Bethlehem, where Jesus Christ was born. You will find that a little ahead, a place of prayer, which is much more on it, which is THE PLACE OF PRAYER WAS ONCE THE STABLE OF AN OX AND AN ASS, WHERE JESUS, MIRROR OF THE WORLD, WAS BORN. He was wrapped in swaddling clothes and laid in a manger between the ox and the ass, just as the Holy Jesus was in the little town of Bethlehem.

Saint Francis, when he was grown, wanted to Bethlehem. Every year, after he had come home, he had a little arrangement which he filled with hay, and he had little animals and images, and pictures of Mary and Joseph and the Baby Jesus, the ox and the ass, the shepherds and the angels; there he knelt and the people at Christmas time; and there he set up the manger, and sang joyful carols beside it. And when Christmas morning came, he said, "God will keep and love dearly all dear you, he stirred the earth for pleasure souls, and gave out doors for the birds, that he believed in at anyone who has an animal, especially a horse or an ox, should give them something special to eat on Christmas Day, because all creatures ought to share in celebrating Jesus' birthday in pleasure God sent.

Having been born like Francis in a stable, Saint Francis felt very close to Jesus, for he always cared to be more like Him than any other man.

Some day, perhaps, you will visit the town of Assisi, in Italy, where Saint Francis was born. You will find there a little chapel, a place of prayer, with an inscription on it which says: THIS PLACE OF PRAYER WAS ONCE THE STABLE OF AN OX AND AN ASS; WHERE FRANCIS, MIRROR OF THE WORLD, WAS BORN. He was wrapped in swaddling clothes and laid in sweet hay between the ox and the ass, just as the baby Jesus was, in the little town of Bethlehem.

Saint Francis, when he was grown, visited Bethlehem. Later, in Italy, after he had come home, he had a little manger built which he filled with hay, and he had little statues made of wood and painted: of Mary and Joseph and the baby Jesus, the ox and the ass, the shepherds and the kings. These he took into the church at Christmas-time, and there he set up the manger scene and lighted candles beside it. And so he started a custom which we still keep and love dearly today. Too, he started the custom of putting seeds and grain outdoors for the birds. And he believed that anyone who has animals, especially an ox or an ass, should give them something special to eat on Christmas Day, because all creatures ought to share in celebrating Jesus' birth and in praising God.

Having been born, like Him, in a stable, Saint Francis always felt very close to Jesus. In fact, he grew to be more like Him than any other man.

The text for SONG OF THE SUN *is from the translation by Matthew Arnold.*